I0844088

Leading Forward: Adaptive Strategies for Tomorrow's Leaders

Jason Dent

Copyright © 2023 Jason Dent

All rights reserved.

ISBN: 9798862220780

DEDICATION

To all the aspiring leaders,

Who, amidst the maelstrom of change, stand steadfast with hope in their eyes and passion in their hearts. To those who wake up every day not just to lead, but to inspire, uplift, and champion the potential in others. This book is a testament to your journey, your resilience, and your unwavering commitment to being the beacon of light in a world that so dearly needs it.

May you always find the strength to push boundaries, the wisdom to listen, and the heart to lead with love and purpose.

Table of Contents

ACKNOWLEDGMENTS

Embarking on the journey of penning this book has been an expedition of introspection, learning, and immense gratitude. The path was strewn with challenges, but every obstacle became an opportunity, thanks to the constellation of remarkable individuals who illuminated my way.

At the forefront of my gratitude is my wife, whose unwavering belief in me provided the strength and perseverance to see this project through. Your encouragement, patience, and love have been the very foundation upon which this work stands.

To my mentors, who have been my guiding stars, imparting their wisdom, challenging my perspectives, and always pushing me to dig deeper — I owe you a debt of gratitude that words can scarcely encompass.

I am indeed indebted to the myriad of leaders and professionals who generously opened up their world to me. Your stories of triumph, setbacks, and invaluable lessons have breathed life and authenticity into these pages. Your openness and trust have been both humbling and inspiring.

My heartfelt thanks go out to my family and friends, who have been my anchors. The countless brainstorming sessions that stretched into the late hours of the night, your endless support, and your unwavering faith in this project have been pivotal.

To each reader who has picked up this book, whether with purpose or serendipity, I extend my deepest appreciation. Your quest for growth, transformative leadership, and meaningful impact is the very soul of this work. It is my sincerest hope that you find in these pages not just information, but inspiration.

Finally, to every individual making ripples of positive change, leading with heart and conviction, know that this book is a celebration of your spirit. It's a testament to the difference one can make, and it's a tribute to leaders like you who make the world a better place.

From the depths of my heart, thank you all.

INTRODUCTION

The New Age Of Leadership

In an era characterized by rapid technological advancements, ever-evolving socio-political landscapes, and a workforce that's more diverse and interconnected than ever before, the paradigm of leadership has been irrevocably transformed. The age of command and control, where leaders ruled from ivory towers, offering edicts to be followed without question, is no more. The new age of leadership demands more than just authoritative direction; it beckons for collaboration, empathy, and adaptability.

In this age, leadership is no longer confined to the corner office. It's a shared responsibility that's distributed across various levels of an organization. The digital age has democratized information, making decision-making a more transparent and inclusive process. As a result, leaders now operate in a milieu where their actions and decisions are constantly under scrutiny, and where their influence is determined as much by their personal integrity and authenticity as by their strategic prowess.

From Tradition To Transformation

Tracing back the arc of leadership through the annals of history, one finds distinct phases that characterize its evolution. Traditional leadership was marked by hierarchical structures. It was an era where position determined power, and the leadership style was largely autocratic. The focus was on efficiency, stability, and the bottom line. The relationship between leaders and their subordinates was purely transactional – a fair day's pay for a fair day's work.

But as the winds of change began to blow, these long-standing tenets started to be challenged. The rise of the knowledge economy, the empowerment of the individual through technology, and the societal shift towards valuing purpose over profit led to the realization that the traditional model was no longer sustainable. The transformation from tradition necessitated a new kind of leadership – one that recognized people as an organization's most valuable asset, that valued emotional intelligence as much as iq, and that understood the importance of purpose, culture, and inclusivity.

The 16 Pillars Of Modern Leadership

Stepping into the limelight of this transformative era are the 16 pillars of modern leadership. These aren't just abstract concepts or lofty ideals; they are practical, actionable principles that can guide leaders in the 21st century. These pillars encompass a range of skills, attitudes, and approaches, from the deeply personal, like emotional intelligence and mindfulness, to the organizational, like agile leadership and a feedback-driven culture.

Together, these pillars represent a comprehensive blueprint for effective leadership in today's complex world. They acknowledge the challenges and uncertainties that modern leaders face, yet also offer hope and guidance. Embracing these pillars doesn't just equip leaders to navigate the present; it prepares them for the future, ensuring that they remain relevant, respected, and effective no matter how the tides of business and society may change.

As we delve deeper into this book, each pillar will be examined in detail, providing insights into its significance, real-world examples of its application, and actionable strategies to embody its principles. From understanding the nuances of ethical dilemmas to celebrating failures as stepping stones to success, these pillars provide a roadmap for leadership that's not just about achieving business outcomes, but about creating a lasting, positive impact on organizations and society at large.

Part I: Emotional & Relational Leadership

1. EMOTIONAL INTELLIGENCE

In today's fast-paced and interconnected world, leadership demands more than just strategic prowess and domain expertise. The spotlight is increasingly on a leader's capacity to understand, harness, and manage emotions, both their own and those of others. This capacity, commonly referred to as Emotional Intelligence (EQ), has emerged as a foundational skill in the repertoire of effective modern leaders.

Definition and Importance:

Emotional Intelligence, as defined by psychologists John Mayer and Peter Salovey, is the ability to recognize, understand, manage, and reason with emotions. It's a step beyond acknowledging emotions, delving deep into the intricacies of emotions' role in thought, decision-making, and interpersonal relationships. Why is EQ so pivotal? Studies consistently show that high EQ can lead to better job performance, leadership skills, mental health, and interpersonal relationships. Leaders with high EQ are adept at conflict resolution, decision-making under pressure, and fostering positive team dynamics. In an era where collaboration, adaptability, and resilience are paramount, EQ stands tall as a significant determinant of leadership success.

Emotions: The Invisible Forces at Work

Emotions aren't just fleeting feelings; they are powerful drivers behind our thoughts, actions, and behaviors. Every decision, from the minutest to the monumental, is influenced by emotions, even when we're not acutely aware of it. For leaders, understanding this emotional undercurrent is crucial. It means recognizing that every team discussion, every organizational change, and every strategic shift resonates on an emotional level with employees. Leaders who fail to acknowledge and address these emotional underpinnings can inadvertently breed discontent, resistance, or apathy. Conversely, leaders attuned to these emotional currents can harness them, channelling positive emotions towards constructive outcomes and mitigating the negative ones before they escalate.

Nurturing EQ: From Awareness to Regulation

The journey to cultivating emotional intelligence begins with self-awareness. Leaders must first introspect, identifying their emotional triggers, understanding their default emotional responses, and discerning the impact of their emotions on their actions. Tools like journaling, mindfulness meditation, and feedback from trusted colleagues can aid this self-exploration.

Once armed with self-awareness, the next step is self-regulation. This doesn't mean suppressing emotions but rather managing them healthily and constructively. Techniques such as deep breathing, pause-before-reacting, and cognitive reframing can help leaders navigate emotional upheavals without being overwhelmed.

Of equal importance is the ability to recognize and respond to the emotions of others. Empathy, often termed as the cornerstone of EQ, enables leaders to perceive the emotional needs and concerns of their team members, fostering an environment of understanding and mutual respect.

EQ in Action: Shaping Positive Work Cultures

Emotionally intelligent leaders don't just impact immediate situations or decisions; their influence permeates the very culture of the organization. Workplaces led by high EQ leaders tend to exhibit higher levels of trust, more open communication, and a palpable sense of community. These leaders handle crises with composure, celebrate successes with genuine joy, and approach challenges with a mix of realism and optimism. They understand that behind every data point, KPI, or strategic objective, there's a human element. By placing emphasis on emotional well-being, understanding, and growth, they foster cultures where employees feel valued, understood, and motivated to give their best.

As the business landscape continues to evolve, leaders will face myriad challenges – from technological disruptions to socio-political changes. While technical skills and domain knowledge will invariably be essential, it's the soft skills, like emotional intelligence, that will determine a leader's ability to steer their teams and organizations towards sustained success. Embracing EQ isn't just about being in touch with one's emotions; it's about creating a ripple effect of positivity, understanding, and resilience throughout the organization.

2. SERVANT LEADERSHIP

A notion once antithetical to the traditional views of leadership has now emerged as one of the most influential and impactful leadership philosophies of our time. This is the approach of Servant Leadership. It's a style that shifts the focus from leading with authority to leading with empathy, service, and empowerment.

Definition and Importance:

Servant Leadership, a term coined by Robert K. Greenleaf in his seminal essay "The Servant as Leader" in 1970, emphasizes the role of the leader as a servant first. Rather than the conventional top-down hierarchy where leaders make decisions and subordinates follow, servant leadership places the needs, growth, and well-being of team members at the forefront. The crux of this philosophy is the belief that when leaders prioritize the holistic well-being and professional development of their team, the entire organization benefits. Why is this important? Because it fosters a culture of trust, collaboration, and mutual respect, which, in turn, boosts morale, increases productivity, and ensures sustainable organizational success.

Leading from Behind: A Paradigm Shift

The essence of servant leadership is often encapsulated by the phrase "leading from behind." Rather than being at the forefront, dictating directions and solutions, servant leaders empower their teams to take the lead. They facilitate rather than command, listen more than they speak, and support rather than dictate. By doing so, they engender a sense of ownership and responsibility among team members, ensuring that they feel valued and integral to the organization's vision and success.

This approach may seem passive or weak to those steeped in traditional leadership models. However, leading from behind requires immense strength, humility, and self-awareness. Servant leaders need to be secure enough to let others shine, wise enough to provide guidance without stifling innovation, and patient enough to allow organic growth and development.

Servants in the Spotlight: Real Stories

Over the years, several influential leaders and organizations have embodied and championed the principles of servant leadership, and their success stories serve as powerful testimonials to its efficacy.

Take, for instance, Howard Schultz of Starbucks. Under his leadership, Starbucks offered health benefits and stock options to part-time employees, a testament to his belief in taking care of his people. Schultz often reiterated that employees, or "partners" as he preferred to call them, were the true heart and soul of the Starbucks brand.

Another exemplar is Herb Kelleher of Southwest Airlines, who believed that the business of business was people. Under his leadership, the airline prioritized employee satisfaction, resulting in remarkably low turnover rates and consistently high customer satisfaction.

These stories highlight that servant leadership isn't just a theoretical concept. It's a practical, impactful, and transformative approach that has driven some of the most successful and beloved organizations in the world.

Becoming a Servant Leader: A Path Forward

So, how does one embark on the journey to become a servant leader? It begins with introspection. Prospective servant leaders must evaluate their motivations, ensuring they genuinely prioritize others' needs over their own ambitions.

Next, it's essential to actively cultivate skills like active listening, empathy, and patience. This can be achieved through formal training, mentorship, and continuous self-reflection.

Additionally, servant leaders must be advocates for a conducive organizational culture. This means championing policies that promote well-being, continuous learning, open communication, and collaboration.

Lastly, aspiring servant leaders must remember that this journey is a continuous one. It demands humility, adaptability, and a genuine love for people.

In an age where business landscapes are ever-evolving and where the human element in organizations is more crucial than ever, Servant Leadership stands out as a beacon, guiding leaders towards an approach that ensures both individual growth and collective success. In serving others, leaders don't diminish their influence or impact; they magnify it.

3. INCLUSIVE LEADERSHIP

In a world that's increasingly globalized and interconnected, leadership demands an understanding and appreciation of diverse perspectives, backgrounds, and experiences. Gone are the days when organizations could thrive within homogeneous bubbles. Today, success is intertwined with the ability to harness diversity and foster an inclusive environment. Enter the realm of Inclusive Leadership.

Definition and Importance:

Inclusive Leadership is the conscious effort by leaders to ensure that all team members feel valued, understood, and empowered to contribute to their fullest potential, irrespective of their race, gender, background, or any other defining characteristic. It goes beyond mere representation; it's about creating an environment where differences are celebrated, voices are heard, and unique perspectives are leveraged. Why is this leadership style so crucial? Because diversity, when coupled with inclusion, leads to innovation, adaptability, and resilience. Organizations that practice inclusive leadership are better equipped to understand global markets, come up with diverse solutions, and navigate the multifaceted challenges of the modern world.

More Than Just Numbers: The Heart of Diversity

When discussing diversity, it's easy to get caught up in statistics – the percentage of women in leadership roles, the representation of ethnic minorities, and so on. While these metrics are essential and indicative, they are just the tip of the iceberg. True diversity goes beyond numbers; it delves into the richness of experiences, perspectives, and ideas that individuals bring to the table.

For instance, a team may have members from various parts of the world. While this geographical diversity is commendable, the real value lies in the varied cultural insights, problem-solving approaches, and worldviews these members bring. Inclusive leaders recognize and celebrate this depth, ensuring that the heart of diversity – its essence and richness – is truly harnessed.

Navigating the Rough Waters of Inclusion

Acknowledging the importance of diversity is one thing; creating an inclusive environment is another. It's a challenging endeavor, fraught with pitfalls. Unconscious biases, deeply entrenched stereotypes, and societal norms can often hinder genuine inclusion. Leaders may, unknowingly, favor voices that resonate with their own, sidelining those that offer dissent or a fresh perspective.

Furthermore, inclusivity is not about agreeing all the time. It's about ensuring that even dissenting voices are heard and respected. Inclusive leaders thus need to strike a balance, fostering an environment where diverse opinions can coexist without leading to fragmentation or discord.

A Playbook for Inclusive Leadership

For leaders aiming to champion inclusivity, here's a playbook to guide the way:

1. **Self-awareness:** Recognize and address your biases. Engage in introspection and be open to feedback.
2. **Active Listening:** Ensure that every voice is heard. Make it a point to solicit opinions from those who might be reticent or overshadowed.
3. **Educate and Train:** Organize workshops and training sessions on diversity and inclusion. Make it a continuous learning process.
4. **Create Safe Spaces:** Encourage open dialogues. Allow team members to express their feelings, concerns, or experiences related to inclusivity.
5. **Celebrate Differences:** Organize events that highlight various cultures, traditions, or experiences. Let diversity be a source of joy and learning.
6. **Empower and Elevate:** Identify and mentor individuals from underrepresented backgrounds. Provide them with opportunities to shine.

Inclusive leadership is more than a buzzword; it's a commitment to excellence, growth, and unity. As the world continues to evolve, so should leadership styles. By embracing diversity in its truest sense and by fostering genuine inclusion, leaders can pave the way for innovative solutions, unparalleled growth, and a harmonious organizational culture.

4. PURPOSE-DRIVEN LEADERSHIP

In the vast sea of businesses, brands, and organizations, what makes a few stand out? Why do some companies not only achieve financial success but also command loyalty, respect, and admiration? Often, the answer lies in their purpose — a purpose that goes beyond profit, touching lives and making a genuine difference. And at the helm of such organizations, you find Purpose-Driven Leaders.

Definition and Importance:

Purpose-Driven Leadership is a leadership style rooted in a clear, compelling purpose or mission that goes beyond business metrics, aiming to make a broader positive impact on society, the environment, or a particular community. Such leaders are not just driven by quarterly profits or stakeholder returns; they are motivated by a deep-seated desire to bring about change, inspire, and make a meaningful difference. Why does this matter? Because purpose acts as a north star, guiding decision-making, fostering employee engagement, and building a strong brand identity. In an era where consumers and employees are increasingly value-conscious, organizations led with a clear purpose tend to outperform their peers, enjoying enhanced brand loyalty, increased employee satisfaction, and sustainable growth.

When Work Meets Passion: The Power of Purpose

The merging of work and passion is a potent combination. When employees feel that their daily tasks align with a larger, meaningful vision, their engagement and productivity often skyrocket. They're no longer just working for a paycheck; they're contributing to a cause, a mission, something larger than themselves. This intrinsic motivation can lead to higher levels of innovation, commitment, and resilience.

Purpose-driven leadership also has a profound external impact. Consumers today are discerning, often choosing to support brands that align with their values and beliefs. A clearly articulated and genuine purpose can differentiate a brand, fostering consumer trust and loyalty.

Organizations with a Heartbeat: A Look Inside

There are numerous organizations worldwide that pulsate with a clear purpose, and their success stories are a testament to the power of purpose-driven leadership.

For instance, consider Patagonia, the outdoor clothing brand. Their mission isn't just about selling clothing; it's about saving the planet. This purpose permeates everything they do, from their sustainable supply chain practices to their commitment to donate a portion of their profits to environmental causes.

Another example is TOMS Shoes. With its "One for One" promise, TOMS commits to donating a pair of shoes for every pair sold. This clear purpose has not only created a loyal customer base but also impacted millions of lives globally.

Crafting a Purpose that Resonates

So, how does one craft a purpose that truly resonates? Here's a guide:

1. Authenticity: Your purpose should stem from genuine care and passion, not just a marketing tactic.
2. Clarity: Ensure your purpose is clear and easily understood. It should resonate with both employees and customers.
3. Alignment: Your organizational practices should align with your purpose. There should be congruence between what you preach and practice.
4. Engagement: Involve stakeholders, especially employees, in the purpose definition process. A collectively defined purpose has higher buy-in.
5. Review and Renew: As the world evolves, it's essential to revisit your purpose, ensuring it remains relevant and impactful.

Purpose-Driven Leadership is not just a leadership style; it's a movement, a paradigm shift that redefines success. In a world that's often driven by numbers, these leaders and their organizations shine bright, reminding us that when purpose and passion align, miracles happen. They inspire us to believe that businesses can be both profitable and purposeful, making the world a better place one decision at a time.

Part II: Adaptive & Responsive Leadership

5. AGILE LEADERSHIP

In a rapidly evolving business landscape, where the only constant is change, leadership styles too must evolve. Leaders can no longer rely solely on top-down hierarchies, rigid strategies, or long-term plans that may become obsolete overnight. Agility — a term once confined to software development and IT — has emerged as a critical leadership trait. This is where Agile Leadership takes center stage.

Definition and Importance:

Agile Leadership refers to the ability of leaders to rapidly adapt to changes in the environment, lead with flexibility, and pivot strategies based on current realities, all while ensuring that the team remains aligned, engaged, and empowered. It's not just about quick reactions; it's about proactively anticipating shifts, fostering a culture of continuous learning, and being resilient in the face of uncertainty. Why is this essential in today's context? Because the pace of technological advancement, market dynamics, and global events has accelerated. Traditional leadership models, which are often reactive and siloed, may fall short. Agile leaders, on the other hand, thrive amidst flux, turning challenges into opportunities and ensuring that their organizations remain ahead of the curve.

The Agile Mindset: Beyond IT Departments

While the term "agile" originated in the realm of software development, emphasizing iterative progress, flexibility, and collaboration, its principles have profound implications for leadership across industries. It's a mindset that emphasizes adaptability, openness to feedback, and a commitment to delivering value.

An agile leader embraces the idea that the best approach might change depending on the circumstances. Instead of rigidly adhering to a set plan, they prioritize outcomes, ready to change tactics if needed. They also understand that leadership isn't just about directing but collaborating. By fostering cross-functional collaboration and open communication, they harness the collective intelligence of their teams.

Keeping Pace in the Fast Lane

In the high-speed highway of modern business, organizations that can't keep up risk obsolescence. Agile leaders ensure their organizations remain dynamic. They cultivate a culture of continuous learning and improvement. Instead of fearing change, they see it as an opportunity for growth.

One of the key principles they adopt is the "inspect and adapt" approach. By regularly reviewing processes, strategies, and outcomes, they glean insights and adjust accordingly. They also promote decentralized decision-making. Instead of bottlenecks at the top, they empower their teams to take decisions, ensuring quicker responses to challenges.

Champions of Change: Agile Leaders in Spotlight

Consider companies like Spotify and Netflix. Their ability to pivot, innovate, and stay ahead in their industries is largely attributed to agile leadership.

Spotify, for instance, uses agile methodologies not just in software development but across its teams. Its organizational structure, with squads, tribes, and guilds, promotes autonomy, alignment, and agility.

Then there's Netflix, which transformed from a DVD-rental service to a global streaming giant. The company's leaders anticipated the shift in consumer preferences and proactively pivoted their business model, exemplifying agility.

Agile Leadership is more than just a buzzword. It's a paradigm shift, emphasizing adaptability, resilience, and proactive evolution. In a world marked by VUCA (Volatility, Uncertainty, Complexity, Ambiguity), agile leaders stand as beacons, guiding their organizations with clarity, conviction, and agility. They not only navigate the turbulent waters of the modern business environment but also harness the waves of change to propel their organizations forward.

6. DIGITAL FLUENCY

As the world finds itself deeply entrenched in the Digital Age, a new type of competency has risen to prominence for leaders and businesses alike: Digital Fluency. This isn't just about using a smartphone or accessing the internet. It's a more profound understanding and capability to navigate, lead, and excel in a digitized environment, ensuring businesses remain competitive and relevant.

Definition and Importance:

Digital Fluency, in a leadership context, refers to a leader's ability to effectively leverage digital technologies to achieve business goals, communicate with varied audiences, streamline operations, and foster innovation. It's more than just digital literacy (knowing how to use digital tools); it's about understanding the strategic implications of these tools and how they can transform businesses. Why is this crucial? As digital transformation accelerates, leaders without digital fluency risk being sidelined, their businesses potentially rendered obsolete. In contrast, digitally fluent leaders are positioned to identify opportunities, mitigate digital-era risks, and drive digital innovation, ensuring their organizations remain at the cutting edge.

Digital Natives, Immigrants, and Explorers

The journey to digital fluency varies depending on one's starting point:

Digital Natives: Often referring to the younger generation, these individuals have grown up in a digital world. For them, navigating digital technologies is second nature. However, fluency for leaders from this group means merging innate digital knowledge with strategic business insights.

Digital Immigrants: This group didn't grow up with digital technology but adapted to it later in life. They might not have the instinctive grasp of digital tools like natives, but with experience, they can achieve a balance between traditional business acumen and the new digital frontier.

Digital Explorers: These are the trailblazers, irrespective of their age, always on the lookout for the next digital innovation. Their leadership style is marked by curiosity, a willingness to experiment, and the ability to drive digital transformation.

The Leadership Tech Stack: Must-Haves

For a digitally fluent leader, understanding the right tech tools—often referred to as the "tech stack"—is paramount. Here are some must-haves for leaders:

Communication Tools: Platforms like Slack, Teams, or Zoom have become indispensable for team collaboration and communication.

Project Management Tools: Tools such as Asana, Trello, or Jira help streamline project workflows and track progress.

Data Analytics Platforms: Being data-driven is vital. Tools like Google Analytics, Tableau, or Power BI help glean insights from data.

Digital Learning Platforms: Continuous learning is key. Platforms like Coursera, Udemy, or LinkedIn Learning ensure leaders and their teams keep updating their knowledge.

Overcoming the Tech Hesitation

Hesitation or resistance to adopt new technologies is not uncommon. However, for leaders, this can be a critical impediment. Overcoming this hesitation involves:

Recognizing the Value: Leaders must understand the strategic value and potential ROI of digital adoption.

Continuous Learning: Leaders should invest time in understanding and learning about new technologies, perhaps by taking courses or attending workshops.

Creating a Supportive Culture: It's vital to foster a culture where experimentation with technology is encouraged, and failures are viewed as learning opportunities.

Seeking Guidance: Mentors, digital experts, or consultants can guide leaders in their digital journey, making transitions smoother.

In this Digital Age, the significance of Digital Fluency for leaders cannot be overstated. It's not just about staying current; it's about leading with vision in a digitized world.

Whether it's harnessing the power of data analytics, implementing AI-driven solutions, or simply fostering a culture of digital innovation, digitally fluent leaders are those who'll steer modern businesses to success, making them   future-ready.

7. HOLACRACY

In the dynamic tapestry of organizational structures, holacracy has emerged as a compelling pattern, challenging traditional hierarchies and championing distributed authority. Yet, like all transformative concepts, it invites both enthusiasm and skepticism. How then do we understand holacracy in its depth, its potential benefits, and its inherent challenges?

Definition and Importance:

Holacracy is a system of organizational governance wherein decision-making power is distributed throughout self-organizing teams rather than being centralized in a management hierarchy. It replaces traditional job titles and descriptions with defined roles, each with its own purpose and accountabilities. The crux is agility, autonomy, and clarity. Why does this matter? As organizations grapple with rapid changes, complex challenges, and the need for innovation, centralized decision-making can become a bottleneck. Holacracy, by decentralizing authority, aims to boost responsiveness, foster innovation, and enhance employee engagement. In essence, it's about empowering everyone to be a leader in their domain.

Tearing Down Walls: A New Organizational

Blueprint

To understand holacracy, envision an organization without its conventional hierarchical pyramid. Instead, imagine concentric circles, each representing a role, with clear accountabilities. These roles are dynamic, evolving based on the work that needs to be done.

Holacracy promotes a "tension-driven" approach. When someone in a role feels a tension – a gap between what is and what could be – they have the authority and responsibility to address it. This ensures that challenges are met head-on, and opportunities are seized swiftly.

Meetings, or "governance sessions," are structured meticulously, ensuring clarity and focus. These sessions are where roles may be redefined, accountabilities adjusted, and policies crafted to guide the work.

Holacracy: A Double-Edged Sword?

While holacracy promises agility and empowerment, it's not without its challenges:

Transition Complexity: Moving from traditional hierarchy to holacracy requires significant shifts in mindset, processes, and structures. This transition can be arduous and unsettling for many.

Potential for Ambiguity: While holacracy seeks clarity, the fluidity of roles can sometimes lead to confusion about who does what.

Cultural Fit: Not every organizational culture aligns with holacracy. Some employees might miss the clarity of a structured hierarchy or feel overwhelmed by the level of autonomy.

Scale Concerns: While small to medium-sized organizations might find it easier to implement holacracy, questions arise about its efficacy in large-scale, global enterprises.

Embracing the Holacratic Movement

For organizations intrigued by holacracy, here are some steps to embrace the movement:

Education: It's vital for leaders and employees to understand the principles and practices of holacracy deeply.

Pilot Implementation: Instead of a wholesale transformation, consider piloting holacracy in a department or project.

Seek Expertise: Engage with experts or consultants who have experience in transitioning to holacratic structures.

Feedback Loops: Regularly gather feedback to understand the challenges and refine the approach.

Commitment: Holacracy requires commitment. It's not just a structural change but a cultural and philosophical shift.

Holacracy, with its bold reimagination of organizational structures, invites leaders and organizations to reflect deeply on their dynamics, challenges, and aspirations. Whether fully adopted, partially implemented, or simply used as inspiration, its principles challenge the status quo, urging a shift towards greater agility, clarity, and empowerment.

8. MINDFULNESS AND PRESENCE

Amidst the whirlwind of deadlines, decisions, and distractions that define the modern corporate landscape, the concepts of mindfulness and presence have emerged as essential anchors, grounding leaders in the midst of chaos. No longer relegated to spiritual or therapeutic arenas alone, mindfulness has cemented its importance in leadership spheres, offering tools for enhanced decision-making, empathy, and overall well-being.

Definition and Importance:

Mindfulness, at its core, refers to the practice of being fully present and engaged in the current moment, aware of one's thoughts, feelings, and sensations without judgment. Presence is the manifestation of this mindfulness in action—how one shows up, engages, and interacts in any given scenario. Why is this paramount in leadership? Leaders enveloped in the frenetic pace of modern business often find themselves fragmented, their attention splintered between past regrets and future anxieties. This scattershot attention can result in poor decision-making, reduced empathy, and decreased productivity. Mindfulness, by rooting leaders in the present, sharpens focus, enhances emotional intelligence, and fosters a calm, balanced approach to challenges.

The Here and Now: More Than Just a Mantra

The present moment, often termed the "here and now," is the only tangible reality we truly have. While the past offers lessons and the future holds aspirations, actions occur in the present. For leaders, being rooted in the present ensures:

Enhanced Decision-making: Decisions are made based on current, clear observations rather than being clouded by biases or anxieties.

Improved Relationships: Being present allows leaders to genuinely listen and connect with team members, fostering trust and collaboration.

Greater Resilience: Engaging with challenges as they come, rather than ruminating on them, builds resilience and adaptability.

Mindful Practices for Busy Leaders

Incorporating mindfulness into a leader's daily routine needn't involve long meditation sessions (though those can be beneficial). Here are some accessible practices:

Mindful Breathing: Just a few minutes of focused attention on one's breath can center the mind and reduce stress.

Single-tasking: In an era of multitasking, consciously choosing to do one thing at a time can enhance efficiency and reduce errors.

Mindful Meetings: Begin meetings with a minute of silence, allowing participants to arrive mentally and engage fully.

Mindful Walking: Convert short breaks or walks to meetings as opportunities to be present, noticing each step and staying attuned to one's surroundings.

From Stress to Serenity: The Mindful Impact

Leaders who embrace mindfulness often experience profound transformations:

Reduced Stress: Mindfulness practices, by their very nature, activate the body's relaxation response, counteracting the detrimental effects of chronic stress.

Increased Emotional Intelligence: Mindful leaders are more attuned to their emotions and those of others, facilitating better communication and team dynamics.

Enhanced Creativity: A calm, present mind is often more open to novel ideas and innovative solutions, creating a fertile ground for creativity and out-of-the-box thinking.

Better Decision-making: A mindful approach tends to reduce impulsive reactions, allowing for more thoughtful, well-informed choices.

Improved Physical Health: Regular mindfulness practices have been linked to various health benefits, from reduced blood pressure and improved sleep to a strengthened immune system.

Strengthened Leadership Presence: A leader deeply rooted in the present moment exudes a certain gravitas and calm, instilling confidence and trust in their teams.

The Ripple Effect of Mindful Leadership

As leaders cultivate mindfulness and presence, the effects often ripple outwards. Teams and departments begin to mirror these qualities, leading to more harmonious work environments. There's a palpable shift in organizational culture—a move away from reactive, frantic energy towards a more measured, proactive, and calm approach. This not only enhances productivity but also contributes to improved team morale and overall job satisfaction.

The practice of mindfulness, simple in its essence but profound in its impact, equips leaders with the tools to navigate the complexities of the modern business landscape with grace, clarity, and resilience. It's a journey of returning to oneself, over and over again, anchoring in the present, and leading from a place of centered strength.

In essence, the practice of mindfulness and presence in leadership isn't just another trend or tool; it's a transformative philosophy that can redefine how leaders relate to their roles, their teams, and themselves. It's an investment in the deepest sense—not just for better business outcomes, but for a richer, more fulfilling life both within and outside the confines of the workplace.

Part III: Empowerment & Growth Leadership

9. FEEDBACK CULTURE

In a rapidly evolving professional landscape, organizations are recognizing that the old models of performance assessment, dominated by once-a-year evaluations, are insufficient. They neither capture the dynamic nature of today's work nor cater to the needs of a workforce that thrives on continuous learning and growth. A new paradigm is emerging, one where feedback isn't an annual ritual, but a part of the daily rhythm—an ongoing dialogue that fuels both personal and organizational evolution.

Definition and Importance:

Feedback Culture refers to an organizational ethos where open, candid, and constructive feedback is encouraged, sought, and valued at all levels. It's not merely about criticism or praise but about fostering a two-way channel of communication that allows for mutual growth, understanding, and improvement. Such a culture goes beyond formal mechanisms, seeping into everyday interactions, team meetings, project discussions, and more.

Why is fostering a Feedback Culture crucial? Because in its absence, individuals operate in silos of information, often unaware of their strengths, areas of improvement, or how their contributions align with broader organizational goals. In a feedback-rich environment:

Employees Grow: Regular feedback provides employees with insights into their performance, guiding their professional development.

Organizations Innovate: With feedback loops in place, organizations can adapt and innovate more swiftly, staying aligned with market needs.

Relationships Strengthen: Open conversations build trust, reduce misunderstandings, and foster stronger team dynamics.

Beyond the Annual Dread: Feedback Renaissance

Gone are the days where feedback was a dreaded annual ritual, often linked more to appraisals than genuine growth. The new-age feedback is frequent, forward-focused, and fosters a growth mindset. Companies that have transitioned to this model report:

Increased Employee Engagement: When employees feel heard and see their feedback acted upon, they feel valued, leading to higher engagement levels.

Reduced Attrition: With regular feedback, there's less room for surprises or pent-up grievances, reducing reasons for sudden departures.

Enhanced Performance: Continuous feedback often correlates with continuous improvement in performance metrics.

The Feedback Toolkit: Getting It Right

While the intention behind feedback is pivotal, the manner in which it's given can make or break its effectiveness. Here's a toolkit for effective feedback:

Be Timely: Provide feedback close to the event, when memories are fresh.

Be Specific: Avoid vague statements. Highlight specific instances or behaviors.

Focus on Behavior, Not the Person: This reduces defensiveness and focuses the conversation on actionable insights.

Ensure It's Two-Way: Feedback isn't a monologue. Encourage responses and discussions.

Use Technology: Employ feedback software and tools that facilitate regular, structured feedback while ensuring anonymity when needed.

Mastering the Art of Constructive Conversations

Crafting a feedback culture isn't just about offering critiques. It's about mastering the art of constructive conversations, which entails:

Active Listening: Truly hear what's being said without immediately formulating a response.

Asking Open-Ended Questions: This elicits deeper insights and understanding.

3. Being Empathetic: Recognize and validate the emotions behind the words, ensuring that the feedback receiver feels seen and heard.

Balancing Positives with Areas of Improvement: This ensures that the conversation isn't skewed heavily towards criticism but offers a holistic view of performance.

Ending on Actionable Steps: Ensure that each feedback

session concludes with clear, actionable steps for both parties, setting the stage for tangible improvement and growth.

Following Up: Feedback without follow-through can feel empty. Check back in to discuss progress, address any ongoing challenges, and celebrate improvements.

Furthermore, it's worth noting that feedback isn't just a top-down process. Encouraging upward feedback, where employees can share their observations and suggestions about organizational processes, management styles, and other relevant areas, can be transformative. This not only empowers employees, making them feel like valuable contributors to the company's evolution, but also provides leaders with unique insights they might not get otherwise.

Creating a feedback-rich culture requires conscious effort, ongoing commitment, and sometimes, a cultural shift. But the dividends it pays—in terms of individual growth, team cohesion, and organizational excellence—are immense. In today's hyper-competitive business landscape, where adaptability and continuous learning are key, organizations can ill afford to neglect the power of constructive feedback.

a Feedback Culture is not just a modern trend but a foundational pillar for any organization aiming to stay relevant, agile, and innovative in the 21st century. It provides the lens through which companies can continually refine their strategies, processes, and people dynamics, ensuring that they are always moving forward, always evolving.

10. CONTINUOUS LEARNING

In today's VUCA (Volatile, Uncertain, Complex, and Ambiguous) world, the pace of change is unprecedented. The knowledge and skills that were once deemed sufficient for a lifetime are now often outdated within a few years, if not months. To navigate this shifting landscape, individuals and organizations alike are recognizing the pivotal role of continuous learning. It's not just about survival but thriving in a world where the only constant is change.

Definition and Importance:

Continuous Learning refers to the ongoing, voluntary, and self-motivated pursuit of knowledge and skills, both for personal and professional development. Unlike traditional learning that often ends with formal education, continuous learning is a lifelong journey that extends beyond classrooms and structured environments.

Why is Continuous Learning paramount? Here are the key reasons:

Adaptability: In a rapidly changing world, continuous

learners are better equipped to adapt, pivoting their skills and knowledge to meet emerging challenges and opportunities.

Competitive Advantage: For organizations, fostering a continuous learning culture can be a significant differentiator, leading to innovation, improved performance, and market leadership.

Personal Fulfillment: For individuals, continuous learning can lead to increased satisfaction, a sense of purpose, and broader life perspectives.

The Unquenchable Thirst for Knowledge:

The core of continuous learning lies in a deep-rooted curiosity—a thirst for knowledge that isn't quenched by degrees or job titles. It's a mindset where every experience is an opportunity to learn, every challenge a lesson in disguise. Continuous learners often exhibit traits like:

Open-mindedness: They're open to new ideas and can change their opinions when presented with new information.

Resilience: They perceive failures as learning opportunities and bounce back with renewed vigor.

Proactivity: They don't wait for learning opportunities to come their way; they seek them out.

Fostering a Culture of Curiosity and Growth:

Building a continuous learning culture in an organization involves more than just offering training programs. It's about creating an ecosystem that values and rewards curiosity, exploration, and growth. Some steps organizations can take include:

Provide Access to Learning Resources: This could range from online courses and workshops to books and seminars.

Encourage Knowledge Sharing: Foster platforms and forums where employees can share insights, lessons, and experiences.

Recognize and Reward Learning: Celebrate those who upskill, reskill, and share their knowledge.

Create Safe Spaces for Failure: Innovation and learning often come with risks. Create environments where calculated risks are encouraged, and failures are viewed as learning experiences.

The ROI of Learning: Beyond Dollars and Cents:

While the tangible returns on investment (ROI) in learning initiatives—like increased productivity, innovation, and revenue—are essential, the intangible benefits can be even more impactful. These include:

1. Enhanced Employee Morale: Employees feel valued when organizations invest in their growth.

2. Attraction and Retention of Talent: In a competitive job market, companies that prioritize learning and development initiatives are more attractive to potential hires and tend to have lower turnover rates. Job seekers and existing employees view these organizations as places where they can grow, evolve, and realize their full potential.

3. Cultivation of Leadership: Continuous learning cultivates future leaders. When employees are exposed to varied experiences and knowledge, they develop a holistic view of the organization, industry, and market, priming them for leadership roles.

5. **Improved Team Dynamics:** As employees learn together, they foster camaraderie, mutual respect, and better collaboration, leading to more cohesive teams.

5. Future-Proofing the Organization: In an era defined by technological advancements and unpredictable market dynamics, organizations that prioritize continuous learning are better positioned to anticipate, adapt, and capitalize on future trends.

In summary, the importance of Continuous Learning cannot be overstated. In the words of the renowned futurist, Alvin Toffler, "The illiterate of the 21st century will not be those who cannot read and write, but those who cannot learn, unlearn, and relearn." Both individuals and organizations need to embrace this philosophy, recognizing that in the journey of continuous learning, the destination is, in fact, the journey itself. Every day presents an opportunity to know more, to be more, and to make a more significant impact. Embracing a continuous learning mindset is not just about professional growth; it's a commitment to personal evolution, ensuring that we're always moving forward, perpetually poised on the cusp of the next breakthrough.

11. FLEXIBLE WORKING

The landscape of work has undergone profound transformations over the last decade. With the confluence of technological advancements, evolving employee expectations, and more recently, global challenges like the COVID-19 pandemic, the concept of a traditional office-bound 9-to-5 job is being steadily eroded. At the forefront of this revolution is the flexible working model—a paradigm shift that promises both challenges and unparalleled opportunities.

Definition and Importance:

Flexible Working refers to any work arrangement that deviates from the conventional work patterns, providing employees with choices regarding where, when, and how they work. This can include arrangements such as remote work, flextime, compressed workweeks, and job sharing, to name a few.

Why is Flexible Working vital in today's landscape? Here's a deep dive:

Employee Well-being and Satisfaction: By providing employees the freedom to design their work schedules around their personal lives, organizations can significantly boost morale, reduce burnout, and improve overall job satisfaction.

Access to a Global Talent Pool: The geographic constraints that traditionally limited hiring are dismantled, allowing organizations to source the best talent from anywhere in the world.

Enhanced Productivity: Contrary to some misconceptions, multiple studies suggest that flexible working can lead to increased productivity, as employees often work during their peak energy periods and face fewer office-related distractions.

Sustainability and Cost Efficiency: With fewer employees commuting daily and reduced need for expansive office spaces, the carbon footprint decreases, and operational costs can drop.

The Rise of the Digital Nomads:

Digital nomads—professionals who work remotely and lead a nomadic lifestyle—are perhaps the most vivid manifestation of the flexible working revolution. Empowered by technology and unbound by location, these individuals blend work and travel, often shifting between co-working spaces, coffee shops, and even exotic locales as they deliver on their professional commitments. Their existence underscores the fact that for many roles, physical presence is no longer a prerequisite for productivity and impact.

Remote Leadership: Challenges and Triumphs:

Leading a remote or flexible team brings its own set of unique challenges. These range from building and maintaining trust, ensuring clear communication, fostering team cohesion, to measuring productivity. However, with the right tools and strategies, these challenges can be transformed into triumphs. Successful remote leadership involves:

Regular Check-ins: Consistent communication is pivotal. This ensures that employees feel connected, valued, and aligned with organizational goals.

Leveraging Technology: Tools like video conferencing, collaborative software, and task management systems can bridge the geographical divide, fostering real-time collaboration.

Building a Culture of Trust: Micromanagement can be the death knell for remote teams. Instead, emphasizing results and trusting employees to manage their tasks and time can foster a sense of ownership and responsibility.

Striking the Perfect Balance:

While the advantages of flexible working are manifold, it's essential to strike a balance. Not all roles may be suited for remote work, and not all employees may thrive outside a structured office environment. Moreover, the lines between personal and professional life can blur in a full-time remote setting, leading to potential burnout. Organizations need to be cognizant of these challenges and adopt a hybrid approach, perhaps, blending traditional office setups with flexible options.

In conclusion, Flexible Working is not just a fleeting trend but a seismic shift in how we perceive and engage with work. It presents a vision of the future where work is not a place you go to but something you do—a future where organizations are more resilient, employees more fulfilled, and the boundaries of what's possible continually expanding.

12. HEALTH AND WELL-BEING FOCUS

In an era of ceaseless hustle, 24/7 connectivity, and burgeoning workplace demands, the significance of health and well-being cannot be overstated. While historically, companies might have confined their employee wellness programs to annual health check-ups or sporadic gym memberships, there's an emergent understanding today that true well-being encompasses much more.

Definition and Importance:

Health and well-being, in the context of the modern workplace, refers to a holistic approach that addresses not just the physical health of employees but also their mental, emotional, and social well-being. This integrative view recognizes that for employees to perform at their best, all facets of their well-being must be nurtured.

Why is a focus on Health and Well-being pivotal?

Boosted Productivity: A physically and mentally healthy employee is invariably more productive. They are likely to have better focus, increased stamina, and fewer sick days.

Enhanced Morale and Engagement: Employees who feel cared for and supported in their health and wellness goals exhibit higher job satisfaction, greater loyalty, and elevated levels of engagement.

Attracting and Retaining Talent: Offering comprehensive well-being programs can be a significant draw for prospective employees and a retention tool for current ones.

Reduced Healthcare Costs: By investing in preventative health and wellness programs, companies can potentially save on more significant health care expenditures in the future.

The Full Spectrum of Employee Wellness:

It's essential to recognize that well-being isn't merely the absence of disease or discomfort—it's a full spectrum that encompasses physical, mental, emotional, and social facets.

Physical Well-being: This includes regular exercise, a balanced diet, adequate sleep, and regular medical check-ups.

Mental and Emotional Well-being: Stress management, mental health support, counseling services, and initiatives that address burnout fall under this category.

Social Well-being: Building healthy relationships at work, fostering a sense of community, and promoting work-life balance are critical components.

Initiatives that Make a Difference:

Today's most progressive companies have taken proactive measures to enhance employee well-being:

Flexible Work Arrangements: As discussed earlier, this aids in achieving a better work-life balance.

On-site Amenities: These can range from fitness

centers and yoga classes to meditation rooms.

Mental Health Support: Offering access to therapists, helplines, or apps that promote mental well-being.

Nutritional Programs: Providing healthy snacks, organizing nutrition workshops, or even having dietitians on-call can make a substantial difference.

Healthy Employees, Thriving Businesses:

When employees thrive, so do businesses. Healthy employees tend to be more creative, better problem solvers, and are generally more pleasant to work with. Furthermore, there's a ripple effect; when one team member prioritizes health, it can inspire others to follow suit, creating a culture of well-being.

Moreover, in a world where businesses frequently face external challenges and uncertainties, having a resilient and well-equipped workforce can be a game-changer. By fostering a culture where health and well-being are at the forefront, businesses are not just investing in their employees but also ensuring their organization's long-term sustainability and success.

In summary, the shift from viewing employees as mere assets to recognizing them as holistic beings—with needs, aspirations, challenges, and strengths—marks a new epoch in the corporate world. By placing health and well-being at the core of their ethos, companies are paving the way for a brighter, healthier, and more prosperous future.

Part IV: Transparent & Ethical Leadership

13. TRANSPARENT LEADERSHIP

In the realm of leadership, the word "transparency" has rapidly shifted from a buzzword to a core expectation. The age of information has ushered in a renewed demand for openness, honesty, and visibility, not just externally to customers and stakeholders, but crucially, internally within organizations.

Definition and Importance:

Transparent leadership refers to the approach wherein leaders communicate openly, share their thought processes, are upfront about the challenges they face, and are honest about the state of affairs within the organization. It's a leadership style that does away with closed doors and silos, in favor of candor, authenticity, and accessibility.

Why is Transparent Leadership so indispensable?

Trust-Building: At its core, transparency breeds trust. When employees feel they're in the loop, they develop greater confidence in leadership and the company's direction.

Enhanced Employee Engagement: Transparency fosters a sense of ownership and belonging among employees, making them more invested in their roles and the organization's mission.

Problem-Solving and Innovation: Open communication channels often lead to collaborative problem-solving and innovative solutions arising from diverse inputs.

Reduced Rumors and Misinformation: In the absence of official communication, rumors can thrive. Transparent leadership counters this by providing clear and accurate information.

Leading in Glass Houses: The New Normal

In the digital age, leaders often find themselves in "glass houses" where actions, decisions, and even mistakes are visible not just to their immediate teams but to the wider world. It's a challenging reality, but it also offers opportunities:

Accountability: The inherent visibility ensures leaders are more accountable for their decisions, fostering responsibility and integrity.

Humanizing Leadership: Seeing leaders navigate

challenges, admit to mistakes, and work towards solutions can humanize them, making them more relatable to their teams.

Real-Time Feedback: The immediacy of today's communication means leaders can receive and act on feedback more swiftly than ever before.

Navigating the Murky Waters of Transparency

However, transparency isn't without its challenges. How much information is too much? How does one balance between being open and overloading teams with information?

Strategic Transparency: It's about being open without causing unnecessary alarm or stress. For instance, while it's essential to communicate potential challenges, it's equally vital to provide solutions or strategies to navigate them.

Protecting Sensitive Information: While the aim is openness, there are matters, especially pertaining to personnel or financial specifics, that might need to be handled with discretion.

Managing Misinterpretations: Clear communication is key. Misinformation or misinterpretation can sometimes be worse than no information.

Building a Culture of Trust and Openness

Transparent leadership is not just about occasional open letters or town halls; it's about fostering a culture where:

Feedback is Welcomed: From all levels of the organization.

Decision-Making is Collaborative: Wherever feasible, involve teams in decisions that affect them.

Mistakes are Learning Opportunities: Instead of being shrouded in blame, they're dissected for lessons.

In summary, transparent leadership is more than a practice—it's a philosophy. It recognizes that in today's interconnected and informed world, leadership is not about guarding information but about sharing, learning, and growing together. It's a journey that demands courage, humility, and above all, a deep-seated respect for the collective intelligence and potential of the workforce.

14. ETHICAL LEADERSHIP

In a globalized and intricately interwoven world, the boundaries of what is right or wrong, acceptable or unacceptable, often blur, making it essential for leaders to operate with a strong sense of ethics. Ethical leadership is more than just following the rulebook; it's about defining and adhering to a moral compass, even when the path becomes unclear.

Definition and Importance:

Ethical leadership can be defined as the practice of leading by recognizing and prioritizing the rights and dignity of others. It means making decisions that are not only legally compliant but also morally sound, ensuring fairness, respect, and integrity in all actions.

Why is Ethical Leadership paramount?

Reputation and Credibility: Ethical missteps can lead to irreversible damage to an organization's reputation. In contrast, ethical leadership enhances credibility among stakeholders.

Stability and Sustainability: Ethical organizations tend to have lower risks of legal and compliance issues, leading to more stability and long-term success.

Employee Morale and Retention: Employees are more likely to be committed and motivated when they believe they are part of an organization with strong moral values.

Stakeholder Trust: Ethical practices foster trust with customers, investors, and other stakeholders, often translating into better business relationships and outcomes.

The Moral Compass in a Complex World

In the vast sea of global business, the moral compass is the north star guiding leaders. It often goes beyond the written code of conduct:

Personal Integrity: An ethical leader's actions mirror their words, ensuring authenticity in leadership.

Empathy: Recognizing the feelings and rights of others, be it employees, customers, or communities, and ensuring no harm in pursuit of business goals.

Courage: Standing up for what's right, even when it's the tougher route.

From Scandals to Standards: Ethics in Play

History is littered with cautionary tales of organizations that met their downfall due to ethical lapses. These aren't just stories of greed but also of myopia, where long-term ethical sustainability was sacrificed for short-term gains.

The Costs of Ethical Failures: Beyond financial repercussions, ethical scandals lead to lost trust, tarnished reputations, and diminished moral within teams.

Setting the Tone at the Top: Ethical behavior should be modeled from the highest echelons of leadership. This sets a precedent and expectation for the entire organization.

Ethics Training: Regular training sessions ensure that all employees are aware of the organization's values and ethical expectations.

Resolving Dilemmas: A Guide for Leaders

Leaders often face complex dilemmas where the "right" path isn't clear. In such situations:

Consult and Collaborate: Engage with diverse team members, consider multiple perspectives, and aim for a consensus when possible.

Return to Core Values: When in doubt, always revert to the organization's core values. They often provide clarity in murky situations.

Seek External Counsel: Sometimes, an external perspective, like that of ethicists or industry peers, can offer valuable insights.

To conclude, ethical leadership is the cornerstone of sustainable and respectable organizations. In a world rife with challenges and complexities, it offers a beacon of light, ensuring that businesses not only thrive economically but also contribute positively to the fabric of society. It's a leadership style that demands introspection, resilience, and an unwavering commitment to doing the right thing, no matter the cost.

15. COLLABORATIVE DECISION-MAKING

The phrase "Two heads are better than one" captures the essence of collaborative decision-making. It's a dynamic shift from the traditional top-down approach where only a few at the helm make key decisions. Instead, it embraces a participatory method, involving relevant stakeholders at various levels in the decision-making process.

Definition and Importance:

Collaborative decision-making is a participatory process where multiple individuals or groups come together to make a decision, ensuring that different perspectives, expertise, and experiences influence the outcome. It fosters collective ownership, responsibility, and commitment to the decisions made.

Why is Collaborative Decision-Making crucial?

Diverse Insights: Collaborative decisions tap into a vast pool of experiences, skills, and viewpoints, leading to more comprehensive and well-rounded outcomes.

Increased Buy-In: When individuals participate in decision-making, they are more likely to support and implement the decisions, reducing resistance and pushback.

Risk Mitigation: Collective decision-making often identifies potential challenges and pitfalls early on, leading to better risk assessment and management.

Empowerment and Inclusion: It fosters a sense of belonging, making team members feel valued and integral to the organization.

Beyond the Boardroom: Decisions Demystified

Traditionally, decisions, especially significant ones, were often made behind closed boardroom doors. However, the modern workplace recognizes that valuable insights can come from anywhere:

Decentralized Decisions: Instead of a centralized decision-making body, organizations are empowering smaller teams or units to make decisions relevant to their domains.

Feedback Loops: Regular channels for feedback ensure that decisions are continuously refined based on real-time insights from the ground.

Transparency: By making the decision-making process transparent, organizations build trust and dispel myths and misconceptions.

Collaboration Tools for the Modern Leader

Technology has been a significant enabler for

collaborative decision-making. Here's how:

Digital Platforms: Tools like Slack, Trello, and Microsoft Teams facilitate real-time communication and collaboration across teams and geographies.

Decision Frameworks: Software like Decision Jam or Loomio help streamline the decision-making process, from brainstorming to voting.

Data Visualization: Tools like Tableau or Power BI help represent complex data in understandable formats, aiding in informed decision-making.

Ensuring Every Voice is Heard

Collaborative decision-making is not just about including everyone but ensuring everyone is genuinely heard:

Active Listening: Leaders should practice active listening, ensuring they understand and consider all viewpoints.

Encourage Dissent: An environment where dissent is valued ensures that decisions aren't just echo chambers but genuinely deliberated.

Follow-Up: Post the decision, gathering feedback on the process and outcome ensures continuous refinement and improvement.

In summary, collaborative decision-making is not a mere trend but a necessity in the complex, rapidly evolving modern workplace. It's about leveraging collective wisdom to navigate challenges and seize opportunities, making the organization more resilient, inclusive, and innovative. It's not about giving up control, but about amplifying leadership through shared responsibility and ownership.

16. CELEBRATING FAILURES AS LEARNING OPPORTUNITIES

In a world that's continuously evolving and where innovation is the key to progress, failure is an inevitable stepping stone. The modern leader recognizes the value in these missteps, understanding that they often pave the way for groundbreaking discoveries and revolutionary ideas.

Definition and Importance:

Celebrating failures doesn't mean reveling in mistakes but rather viewing them as valuable learning opportunities. It's about shifting the organizational mindset from one of aversion to one of acceptance, understanding, and growth.

Why is this paradigm shift crucial?

Innovation Catalyst: Every significant invention in history came after numerous failed attempts. By not fearing failure, organizations can push the boundaries of what's possible.

Resilience Building: When teams understand that failures aren't fatal but formative, they develop resilience, recovering faster from setbacks.

Risk Tolerance: An organization that punishes mistakes fosters a conservative mindset, whereas one that celebrates them encourages calculated risk-taking.

Growth Mindset: Viewing failures as learning opportunities instills a growth mindset, promoting continuous improvement and adaptability.

Rewriting the Script on Mistakes

For generations, failures have been stigmatized, often seen as a reflection of incompetence. However, in the landscape of rapid change:

Failure as Feedback: Instead of a dead end, mistakes become feedback mechanisms, guiding course corrections.

Systemic Understanding: Not all failures are due to individual errors. Many arise from systemic issues, and recognizing this helps improve processes and strategies.

Reframing Language: Organizations are switching from punitive language ("Who's responsible for this mistake?") to constructive dialogues ("What can we learn from this?").

From Failures to Frontiers: Stories of Redemption

Throughout history, many success stories arose from the

ashes of failures:

Sir James Dyson took 5,126 attempts before perfecting the first bagless vacuum cleaner.

The Post-it Notes were a result of a failed attempt at creating a super-strong adhesive.

Airbnb founders sold customized cereal boxes to keep their idea afloat when initial traction was minimal.

Such stories not only inspire but remind us that behind every great success, there's often a trail of failures.

Fostering an Innovative and Fearless Culture

For organizations to truly benefit from failures, they must cultivate an environment that supports it:

Psychological Safety: Employees should feel safe to express ideas, ask questions, and even make mistakes without fear of retribution.

Rewarding Attempts: Recognizing and rewarding efforts, not just outcomes, encourage trying and iterating.

Post-Mortem Reviews: Instead of assigning blame, dissecting what went wrong in a constructive manner ensures lessons are extracted and applied in the future.

In essence, celebrating failures is not about being reckless but recognizing the potential that lies within these moments. It's about building organizations that are resilient, innovative, and constantly learning. In the grand tapestry of success, failures are not stains but integral threads that give it depth, character, and strength.

CONCLUSION: LEADING INTO THE FUTURE AND CRAFTING A NEW LEADERSHIP MANIFESTO

Leading into the Future

As we stand on the cusp of a world shaped by rapid technological advancements, social dynamics, and evolving expectations, the mandate for leadership is clear: evolve or risk irrelevance. Leading into the future is not merely about adopting the latest tech trends or jumping onto the newest management fad; it's about recognizing the profound shifts in the way we work, think, and interact.

The age of silos is dissolving. Organizations are becoming flatter, more transparent, and democratic. The 'command and control' structure that was once the hallmark of traditional leadership is now an outdated relic. Instead, a distributed, collaborative, and compassionate form of leadership is rising, where leaders are not just decision-makers but also mentors, facilitators, and learners.

This futuristic leadership demands more than just strategic acumen or decision-making prowess. It's about cultivating an ability to envision far beyond quarterly results, to grasp the ripples of one's actions on society, and to understand the symbiotic relationship between business health and societal well-being. The leader of tomorrow is emotionally attuned, ethically grounded, technologically savvy, and inclusively oriented.

Moreover, as global challenges such as climate change, social inequities, and geopolitical tensions intensify, leaders will be at the frontline of forging solutions. The ability to think systemically, connect the dots, and leverage diverse talents will be indispensable. Leaders will be less 'saviors' and more 'orchestrators,' harnessing the collective might of their teams to address multifaceted challenges.

A New Leadership Manifesto

In light of the shifts and expectations, it's time to craft a new leadership manifesto—a guide that captures the essence of what leadership should embody in this dynamic era:

Purpose Over Profits: While profitability remains crucial, leaders must recognize the broader purpose of their organizations, understanding that long-term success intertwines with the value delivered to society.

Human-Centricity: People are not resources; they are the heart and soul of any organization. The new manifesto places the well-being, growth, and aspirations of people at the center of every organizational decision.

Ethical Grounding: In a world of complexity, the moral compass must be the guiding light. Leaders commit to unwavering ethics, even when faced with the most challenging business dilemmas.

Embracing Diversity: It's not about tokenism but recognizing that diverse teams bring rich perspectives, innovation, and resilience. True leadership seeks, celebrates, and leverages this diversity.

Lifelong Learning: The manifesto acknowledges that the pace of change is so rapid that what worked yesterday might not work tomorrow. Leaders pledge to continuous learning, evolving both in skill and mindset.

Collaboration Over Competition: The challenges of the future are too vast for any one leader or organization to tackle alone. The new leadership champions partnerships, alliances, and shared goals.

Adaptive Resilience: Change is not an event but a constant. The manifesto recognizes this, championing leaders who are not just reactive but also proactive, foreseeing changes and molding them into opportunities.

Transparent Integrity: Leadership no longer hides behind closed doors. Actions are taken transparently, decisions are communicated openly, and mistakes are acknowledged and learned from.

In crafting this new leadership manifesto, we are not

merely setting guidelines but creating a vision. A vision of a world where leadership is not a position but a responsibility—a responsibility to craft better organizations, foster happier employees, and, most importantly, shape a more compassionate, just, and sustainable world.

As we close this exploration of modern leadership, let's not see this as an end but a beginning—a starting point of a journey towards a brighter, more inclusive, and empowered future. The tools, strategies, and philosophies shared are your compass. The next steps, the adventures, the challenges, and the victories are yours to forge.

www.ingramcontent.com/pod-product-compliance
Lightning Source LLC
Chambersburg PA
CBHW061013260726
48661CB00005B/2177